thecove cookbook
...food with a view

Arty Williams

Paperback edition first published in the UK in 2007 by 'the cove'
maenporth beach . nr falmouth . cornwall . tr11 5hn
© 2007 Arty Williams

A catalogue record of this book is available from the British Library.
ISBN 978-0-9557166-0-7

Author: Arty Williams
Project Editor: Madeline Toy
Pastry Chef: Janine Cremore
Book Design: Claire Lipman at Superbella™
Photography: David Griffen

Printed and Bound by R. Booth Ltd, Cornwall

In association with

contents

Foreword

These are some of the things that I remember enjoying to eat whilst growing up; egg mayonnaise sandwiches were top of the list, preferably with just warm egg; belly pork and sautéed potatoes, lamb chops and garras potatoes (a style of savoury braised potato), cauliflower cheese, the list goes on… Apart from a good prawn cocktail and a fillet of mackerel, I only ate fish occasionally. Cod, pollack and lemon sole, always very simply grilled or pan fried, I remember most.

My favourite roast meal was definitely roast duck – I'm a leg man myself… I always ate this with my fingers and really got stuck in. One Sunday evening, I was probably around 12 years old, so excited about my roast duck and really hungry I picked up the duck leg and launched my teeth into it, biting straight through my tongue.

How the hell did I get here? I grew up in Falmouth mainly spending my summers sailing and my winters playing rugby. Apart from those things, not a lot else mattered to me. As a child I was employed by school – at least, that's how it felt. An adventurous young fella whose hand always went up first when it came to earning a few quid, whether it was delivering leaflets, cleaning people's gardens, anything for some financial freedom. I left school and was promptly escorted to Cornwall College by my parents, wrestling with their ideas and ensuring them that I would go and get myself a job. However, attending college full time and graduating from the wash up at a good hotel, I started work as a commis veg chef. Although I enjoyed a busy kitchen environment, nothing really clicked with me at this stage, so I had myself a department swap and started waiting on tables in the restaurant. Basically, this suited my sailing and rugby interests as it was easier to get time off.

In and out of various jobs and not really settling anywhere, I decided to travel around New Zealand cooking and playing rugby. It was here that I learnt more about contemporary food from an international perspective by working outside of Cornwall in the cities of Auckland and Wellington. At this time, I realised that my skills in the kitchen were strong and that I had a firm understanding of how a quality kitchen should run.

I found my passion for food when I took a job at Jordans International Seafood Restaurant in the hub of Sydney's Darling Harbour. What I learnt here was that food cooked with creativity, vision and imagination can provide a testament to my love of a landscape rich in both beauty and the finest ingredients. This was to launch my career. If only I could get a head chefs position when I returned to Cornwall…

A vast repertoire of modern food was stored in the back of my mind and I wasn't willing to unleash it until I was head chef. Twelve months later, the opportunity arose. I proceeded to open two new restaurants as head chef, both were very successful and I worked extremely hard to build myself a solid reputation.

At 29 years old I had the chance to open my own restaurant, 'the cove'. With sea views over Falmouth Bay and a beautiful white sandy beach, this was the perfect venue for the way that my career had developed. I am able to provide light fresh and zingy flavours in summer and more deep, rich and traditional tastes in winter. 'the cove' has become the final and most challenging leg of my career to date, but by far the most enjoyable. It is a constant juggle between running a busy kitchen and restaurant and keeping the business advancing alongside all the usual demands of day-to-day work, but ultimately portraying an enthusiasm and passion for cooking that does not waver.

This cookbook is a reflection of the development of 'the cove's' kitchen over the last 5 years, alongside the cornerstone of 'the cove's' philosophy, that food should be enjoyed… and the secret…simple food, cooked well. I hope that reading this book will inspire you to cook, to share in my passion and to bring some of the unique 'cove' atmosphere to the most mundane of days. I have kept the recipes simple, yet flavoursome, giving you as much chance to use as much of the cookbook as possible. My aim being, that you create more meals and dinner parties from this cookbook than any other cookbook on your shelf.

Enjoy, experiment & be inspired to cook…

Our aim with this collection of recipes, compiled by award-winning chef Arty Williams, is to represent the very best of contemporary Cornish cookery.

'the cove' is a stylish restaurant a few miles out of Falmouth towards the Helford River, nestled in the valley at Maenporth Beach it boasts predictably beautiful views.

Since opening 'the cove' in 2002, Arty's high standards, but down to earth principles, have created a restaurant where the service, wine & food is refined & taken seriously, yet the ambience is casual and relaxed.

Continuing to provide quality innovative food from the freshest of local ingredients, the constantly changing menu, that specialises in locally caught fish but also offers vegetarians great options, will sustain your interest throughout. 'the cove' maintains a sharp focus on locally produced food and the promotion of quality Cornish ingredients.

'the cove' is a great location at any time of day or year. Whether you would like a special meal, a light snack (the fabulous tapas menu is perfect if a mid week drink in the sun can be negotiated!), a leisurely drink at the bar or a coffee after a stroll along the beach and cliffs...'the cove' has it all.

Tapas

Mozzarella and Basil Stuffed Figs
wrapped in Parma ham with honey and lemon dressing

Serves 4

8 figs
8 slices of Parma ham
2 buffalo mozzarella balls
12g torn basil leaves
juice of 1 lemon
honey
olive oil
seasoning

Cube the mozzarella balls and place into a bowl with the basil, season and drizzle with olive oil. Cut each fig in a criss cross from the top down by 1/3. Separate the 4 quarters at the top of the fruit. Stuff the mozzarella mix into the top of the figs. Wrap the stuffed figs with Parma ham securing the ends tightly.

Pour the lemon juice into a small bowl, add the same amount of honey and double the quantity with olive oil. Whisk well and drizzle onto stuffed figs.

Roast in a medium hot oven for 10 minutes until just cooked. Serve with salad and fresh bread.

Spicy Lamb Koftas
with Tzatziki

Serves 4

500g minced lamb
1/2 finely chopped red onion
3 crushed garlic cloves
1/2 finely chopped fresh red chilli
25g chopped basil
25g chopped mint
10g finely chopped ginger
1 tbsp soy sauce
seasoning
8 cocktail sticks

Garnish | shredded iceberg lettuce
cubed cucumber
sliced spring onions
2 pitta bread

Tzatziki | 50g finely chopped cucumber
2 crushed garlic cloves
10g chopped mint
1 tsp sugar
100g sour cream
juice of 1/2 lemon

Lamb Koftas
Mix all of the above ingredients in a bowl until bound together. Roll out into 24 small balls with the diameter of a 2 pence piece. Place 3 balls onto each cocktail stick. Grill each lamb kofta, turning regularly, until cooked.

Garnish
Quarter the pitta breads and grill each side until golden brown. Place shredded iceberg lettuce, cubed cucumber and sliced spring onion onto the bread and place 2 koftas on top of each quarter.

Tzatziki
Mix together all of the tzatziki ingredients. Top the lamb koftas with the tzatziki.

Naturally Smoked Cornish Haddock Fillet
with mediterranean vegetables and parmesan cream sauce

Serves 4

300g smoked haddock
1 courgette
1/2 aubergine
1 small red onion
1/2 red pepper
1/2 green pepper
1/2 yellow pepper
50ml white wine
200ml whipping cream
20g grated parmesan
seasoning

Haddock

Cut smoked haddock into 4 equally sized portions. Place a tbsp of water on a grill pan to help create some steam. Place the haddock fillet, skin side up, onto the grill pan and place under the grill. Grill for approximately 6-7 minutes, carefully remove the skin and turn the fillet over. Return to the grill until cooked through.

Mediterranean Vegetables

Cut each vegetable into roughly 1cm square cubes and fry in a pan until just softened with a slight bite.

Parmesan Cream Sauce

Place white wine into a saucepan and reduce by 1/2. Add whipping cream and parmesan and season. Reduce until the sauce is bubbling and thickened.

Place the mediterranean vegetables on the centre of your plate and top with the haddock. Coat generously with your parmesan cream sauce & serve immediately.

Falmouth Bay Oysters
grilled with bacon and Worcestershire sauce

Serves 1

6 fresh Falmouth Bay Oysters - per person
3 rashers of bacon
Worcestershire sauce
freshly cracked black pepper
1 oyster knife

Firstly you need to shuck the oysters. *You could get this done for you where you buy your oysters, but freshly opened oysters only have a shelf life of 2 to 3 hours.*

Place the closed oyster flat side up with the round edge towards the palm of your hand. Have a thick cloth between your palm and the oyster for safety. Place the knife into the back corner of the oyster unhinging the top from the base. When the knife pierces the oyster, scrape across the top flat edge of the inside of the oyster to remove the meat from the shell. Remove the top of the shell. Gently remove the oyster from the base of the shell by scraping the oyster knife in and around the meat. The oyster will now be loose and sitting in half of the shell.

Place the oysters, in their shells, on a flat grilling tray. Remove excess fat from the bacon rashers and finely slice. Place the bacon on top of the oysters, drizzle with Worcestershire sauce and lightly sprinkle with black pepper. Grill until the bacon is cooked and the oyster is warmed through. Serve immediately.

To serve your oysters naturally, simply open, squeeze fresh lemon juice and sprinkle with freshly cracked black pepper. Enjoy straight away.

...lemon and freshly cracked black pepper is, in my opinion, the best way to enjoy an oyster...

14

'the cove' Summer Hummus Dip ...*not a chickpea in sight!!*

400g feta cheese
4 large crushed garlic cloves
150g large black olives
50g finely chopped fresh mint leaves
1 large lemon
20g sugar
350ml sour cream
seasoning

Crumble the feta into a mixing bowl. De-stone and roughly chop the olives. Add the olives, mint, garlic, sugar and seasoning. Squeeze in the juice of the lemon and bind together with the sour cream.

Serve with fresh, chunky bread or toasted pitta bread.

Extras

Olive Marinade

red chilli	lime zest & juice
red onion	olive oil
mint	seasoning
coriander	

The main ingredients for me are the chilli & mint, so I would make these the strongest flavours…

'the cove' Green Salad

lettuce leaves – of your choice	kiwi fruit
spring onions	coriander
mange tout	mint
avocado	passion fruit
grapes	

Chop the ingredients & toss together in a large mixing bowl with mustard dressing (see page 42). Top your salad with fresh raspberries and blackberries.

…you will feel great after a bowl of this fresh, zingy salad…

Lunch

Roasted Flat Field Mushrooms
with Carn Brea goats cheese, deep fried potato and leeks and sweet red onions

Serves 4   8-12 flat field mushrooms – depending on size
250g Carn Brea goats cheese
1 leek
1 grated potato
sweet red onions (see page 30)
flour for dusting
seasoning
vegetable or sunflower oil - for deep frying
butter

Deep Fried Leek and Potato
Cut the leek into thin strips and coat lightly with seasoned flour. Deep fry for 30-40 seconds in very hot oil until golden brown. Drain on kitchen towel. They will crisp up once cooled. Soak the grated potato in cold water to remove the starch. Drain well and deep fry for 40-50 seconds until golden brown. Drain on kitchen towel.

Mushrooms
Place a knob of butter on top of each mushroom and drizzle with olive oil. Season the mushrooms and roast in a medium hot oven until they are just cooked. Use 2-3 mushrooms per portion depending on size. Once cooked, top each portion evenly with the Carn Brea goats cheese and roast (or grill) until just melted. Top with the deep fried leek and potato and warm sweet red onions.

Serve with salad, potatoes or vegetables of your choice.

Student Option
Use your favourite packet of crisps as the crunchy centre of this dish – to replace the deep fried leek and potato.

...one of the best-ever selling vegetarian dishes at 'the cove'. It can be served as a starter, lunch or tapas dish, a firm favourite.

Cornish Mackerel Fillets
with new potatoes, cherry tomatoes, rocket and pesto butter

Serves 4

8 large mackerel fillets (pin boned)	**Pesto Butter** 10g pinenuts
600g new potatoes	10g garlic
250g cherry tomatoes	10g parmesan cheese
100g wild rocket	50g basil
100g seedless grapes	50g spinach
olive oil	125g softened butter
seasoning	ground pepper

Blend the pinenuts, garlic, parmesan and a large pinch of pepper in a food processor. Then add the spinach and basil, blend again. Finally add the butter and mix well. Roll into a sausage shape, wrap in cling film and refrigerate.

Boil new potatoes until cooked, strain and cut into quarters. Halve the cherry tomatoes, mix in a bowl with olive oil and seasoning. Place the tomatoes in a roasting tray and put in a medium hot oven to soften. Toss the warm potatoes and tomatoes in a mixing bowl with the grapes and rocket. Divide between 4 plates.

Drizzle the mackerel fillets skin side up with olive oil and seasoning. Place under the grill until the skin starts to crisp. Cut 8 slices of pesto butter and place one onto each mackerel fillet. Place under the grill until almost melted. Remove from the grill and place 2 mackerel fillets, skin side up, on top of your potato and tomato mix. Drizzle any remaining butter around the plate.

...prepare your pesto butter and new potatoes the day before so there is hardly anything to do. This dish is a tasty light lunch, perfect for those summer days in the garden...

Seafood Potato Cakes
with pancetta and a runny poached egg

Serves 4

750g peeled potatoes	100g smoked haddock
3 large finely chopped shallots	100g mackerel
25g drained & chopped capers	100g cod
10g chopped parsley	(all fish should be cooked, drained and skinned)
10g chopped tarragon	100g peeled prawns
10g chopped coriander	breadcrumbs
10g chopped watercress	seasoning
1/2 tsp English mustard	8 thinly sliced slices of pancetta
1 egg yolk	4 poached eggs

Boil or steam potatoes until cooked through. Mash the potatoes when dry, but still warm. Add shallots, capers, herbs, watercress, mustard and egg yolk to the potatoes and mix thoroughly. Add the fish and prawns. Mix and season well. Slowly add breadcrumbs until mixture will hold its shape. To make up the seafood cakes, divide the mixture into 4 and roll into a tennis ball size, then slightly flatten. Place in the refrigerator on a lightly floured tray until required.

Heat oil in a frying pan and cook cakes until lightly brown on both sides. Place them in a medium hot oven for about 15-20 minutes until they are hot in the centre. Place the pancetta under the grill until lightly cooked.

To serve, top the seafood potato cakes with 2 slices of pancetta and a runny poached egg.

With the seafood potato cakes, anything goes… any fish or shellfish can be used, create your own flavours. The potato varieties change throughout the year which means you will probably use a different amount of breadcrumbs every time you make these cakes.

…I can suggest different toppings such as ham/bacon and cheese; seared scallops and a cream sauce; basil roasted vine tomatoes, sour cream and sweet red onions to name but a few!

Slow Roast Marinated Belly Pork
with stir fried bok choi

Serves 4

1/2 pork belly (boned and skinned)
2 bok choi
1/2 large finely sliced red onion
4 large oyster mushrooms
100g fine beans
chicken stock
seasoning
olive oil
large knob of butter

Marinade

500g tomatoes (blanched and peeled)
1 red chilli*
2 star anise*
1 pinch cloves*
20g ginger*
4 cloves garlic*
60g demerara sugar*
25g coriander (with stalks)
seasoning*
20ml oyster sauce
20ml soy sauce

Marinade
Place all dry* ingredients into a blender and blend. Add all other ingredients and blend further to create as fine a marinade as possible.

Preparing Pork
Make diagonal incisions across the skin side and underbelly of the pork. Rub in the marinade and leave for at least 1 hour. After this rub in more marinade and place on a wire roasting rack in a roasting tray. Cover the bottom of the roasting tray with water ensuring it does not touch the meat. Roast for 20 minutes at 180°C then for 2 1/2 - 3 hours at 120°C. Leave to rest for 20 minutes. Slice the pork and layout on a grill pan. Brush with more marinade and grill or roast until hot.

Stir fry
Quarter the bok choi and remove the root. Halve the mushrooms. Top, tail and blanch the fine beans. Heat a frying pan with a drizzle of olive oil. Sauté the bok choi and mushrooms for 2 minutes. Add the red onions and fine beans and cook for a further 2 minutes. Moisten with chicken stock and season. Add butter until melted and serve immediately topped with 3 slices of your slow roasted belly pork.

Cornish Fillet Steak Sandwich
with smoked bacon, avocado and Westcountry brie

Serves 4

500g fillet steak
12 rashers of smoked bacon
1 ripe avocado
200g Westcountry brie
120g sunblushed tomatoes
100g rocket
4 large ciabatta rolls
butter

A Sandwich fit for a King

In a hot frying pan, seal the fillet steak, place in the oven and cook to your liking (I recommend nice and pink). Grill the bacon and set to one side. Quarter the avocado, skin and slice. Cut the brie into 8 chunky strips. Place the ciabatta in the oven to warm through. Slice the fillet steak and divide into 4 portions on a grilling tray. Place 3 rashers of bacon onto each portion of steak, followed by 1/4 of the avocado and place under the grill to warm through. Remove the bread from the oven and spread with butter. Top with the rocket and sunblushed tomatoes. Place 2 strips of brie onto each portion of steak and grill until melted. Place onto the bread and serve immediately.

…any steak can be used but sometimes combinations of food were meant to be. Watch that greedy ciabatta soak up those juices…

Extras

Sweet Red Onions

2 sliced red onions	1 tbsp apricot jam
150ml red wine	juice & zest of 1 lemon
3/4 tbsp redcurrant jelly	1/2 tbsp demerara sugar

Place all of the ingredients, except the red onions, into a saucepan. Reduce the liquid until syrupy & sticky. Add the red onions & turn the heat to low. Stir well & cover. After 10 minutes remove the lid & cook further until the mixture is sticky & sweet.

…these sweet red onions are really versatile, they can be kept in a jar in the fridge & used in many dishes. The onions make a great topping for fish & meat, taste fantastic in vegetarian parcels & tarts, & also gives pasta dishes instant flavour…

Basic Pasta Recipe

125g pasta flour – or strong flour	olive oil – a glug!
1 egg	seasoning
1 egg yolk	flour to dust

Sieve flour onto a clean work surface. Make a dip in the centre of the flour, then add the eggs, seasoning & olive oil. Bring the flour from the sides into the centre. Mix until it forms a soft dough. Lightly flour your work surface & consistently work the dough for 5-10 minutes. Wrap the dough in cling film. Now the pasta dough needs to be rested for at least 20 minutes in the fridge.

Pasta Verde (Green Pasta)| You will need to very slightly wilt 25g spinach in a pan. Squeeze all possible water out of the spinach & chop very finely with a knife, as close to a pulp as you can. Add the spinach to your well, before the eggs. If the pasta dough appears a little wet, just add more flour.

If you have a food processor you can bring together your dough mix in the processor by pulsing the ingredients. For pasta verde, puree the spinach first then make the dough. Unfortunately a food processor doesn't mean you don't have to work the dough for 5-10 minutes. If you have a pasta machine, lovely job. Just remember to put the dough through each setting twice to make it nice & smooth. You can also roll the pasta with a rolling pin, as fine as 2mm. Fresh pasta cooks far, far quicker than dried. Be really careful not to overcook you pasta.

Starters

Pan Seared Falmouth Bay Scallops
with a garlic and olive oil crust, creamy peas and Parma ham

Serves 4

12 plump Falmouth Bay scallops
160g garden peas
12 slices of Parma ham
50ml white wine
150ml whipping cream

60g wild rocket
3 large finely chopped garlic cloves
100ml olive oil
breadcrumbs
seasoning

Garlic and Olive Oil Crust
Add the garlic to a hot pan and fry for 30 seconds without adding colour. Add 2/3rds of the olive oil and warm through. Take off heat and mix in the breadcrumbs until full absorbed and crumbly.

Creamy Peas
Bring the white wine to the boil and reduce by 1/2. Add the cream and reduce until bubbling and thickened. Season with salt and pepper. Lightly crush peas to release their natural sweetness and add to sauce.

Scallops
On a grilling tray, divide the rocket into 12 portions and place a slice of Parma ham on the top of each portion. Top each rocket and Parma ham stack with a spoonful of creamy peas, the sauce should be very thick by now. In a hot pan, sear the scallops, each side should be golden brown and lightly caramelised, this will take between 1 and 2 minutes. Season each side during searing. Place each scallop on top of the creamy peas and place under a hot grill to warm through. Sprinkle the garlic crust mixture onto each scallop and grill until golden brown. Use a fish slice to remove each portion from the grilling tray.

...my favourite scallop dish, with it's simple flavours and textures. The saltiness of the parma ham, creamy sweet peas and crunchiness of the garlic topping...

Caramelised Red Onion Tarte Tatin
with endive, feta and balsamic salad

Serves 4

250g puff pastry
2 large red onions
demerara sugar
25ml balsamic vinegar
1 small endive
200g feta cheese
50ml olive oil
seasoning

Endive, Feta & Balsamic Salad
Mix the washed endive, feta cheese, balsamic vinegar and olive oil together in a bowl and season.

Caramelised Red Onion Tarte Tatin
Preheat the oven to medium hot. Roll out the puff pastry and cut into 4 circles, each approximately 15cm diameter. Place a frying pan, the same size as the pastry circles, onto a low heat and lightly sprinkle with demerara sugar. Cut the onions into 12 wedges per onion. When the sugar starts to melt, place 6 wedges of red onion into the pan with a splash of olive oil, a drop of balsamic and season. If the sugar appears burnt STOP! clean the pan and begin again.

Place the pastry circles on top of the onions and place the pan in a preheated oven 180°C for approx 8-10 minutes or until the pastry is golden brown. Turn the tarte tatin out so that the onions are on the top. The onions should be caramel glazed and shiny. Place a handful of the salad on top of each tarte tatin. Serve immediately.

Congratulations, you have just produced a French classic…
…guaranteed to impress why not make one large tart and cut into portions, be sure to slightly increase the cooking times. Ideal for a dinner party as each tart can be prepared a few hours in advance and gently reheated in the oven.

Smoked Chicken Salad

Serves 4

3 smoked chicken breasts
12 asparagus spears
1 ripe avocado
100g sunblushed tomatoes
2 spring onions
60g rocket
coriander and chilli oil (see page 42)
seasoning

Blanch the asparagus in boiling salted water until slightly soft. Remove the asparagus from the pan, refresh in cold water and drain. Roughly chop the sun-blushed tomatoes and cut the spring onions into 3cm fine strips. De-stone, peel and slice the avocado. Slice the smoked chicken breasts.

Place all of the ingredients into a large mixing bowl, drizzle with chilli and coriander oil and season with salt and pepper.

This basic, but delicious salad can also be used as a light lunch. Variations could include fresh mixed herbs, a flavoured mayonnaise, a variety of oils and dressings… you could also make a warm salad in the winter by warming the smoked chicken, asparagus and avocado.

…for an ideal Summer BBQ salad, substitute the smoked chicken with char-grilled chicken strips & even replace the rocket with cos lettuce for crunch…

Helford River Mussels
in a white wine and garlic cream sauce

Serves 4

2kg fresh Helford River mussels
100ml white wine
2 large finely chopped shallots
4 crushed garlic cloves
500ml whipping cream
25g fresh chopped parsley
25g fresh chopped tarragon
freshly cracked black pepper

Take time to clean the mussels properly. Discard the beards from the centre of the shells. Even scrape the shell with the back edge of a knife. You will get the benefits with a clean, thick, shiny sauce that grips the mussels and coats them so that they eat perfectly!!

Add the mussels and white wine to a hot pan, cover with the lid and steam until all of the mussels are opened. Move the mussels around the pan to help them open. Remove the mussels from the pan and discard any that are unopened.

Strain the white wine and cooking juices to ensure any stray grit from the shells is removed. Return the liquid to the heat in a clean pan and add the shallots and garlic. Cook for 2 minutes. Season with freshly cracked black pepper and add the cream. Reduce the sauce until it begins to bubble and thicken. Add the parsley, tarragon and the steamed mussels. Toss the mussels in the sauce to fully coat them and make sure they are hot.

Serve with fresh chunky bread.

...the key to good mussels is the sauce. You can't be sure how good your mussels are until they're open. Every fishmonger will tell you that their mussels have "got 'ansome big meat in 'em boy"...

'the cove' Crab Cocktail

Serves 4

250g cooked peeled prawns
250g fresh Newlyn white crab meat
150ml sour cream
juice of 1 lemon
12g chopped chives
mixed lettuce leaves
seasoning

Marie Rose Sauce | 4 tsp mayonnaise
1 tsp tomato ketchup
Worcestershire sauce - to taste
creamed horseradish - to taste
seasoning

Mix all of the marie rose sauce ingredients together.

Take two mixing bowls, in one bowl add the prawns, season with salt and pepper and squeeze over half the lemon juice. In the second bowl mix together the chives, sour cream and the remaining lemon juice.

Divide the lettuce leaves between 4 plates and place a 7cm presentation ring on top of each. Put a level teaspoon of the marie rose sauce into the centre of each ring. Fill each ring with a 1/4 of the prawn mix. Top the prawns with your sour cream mix. Finish your cocktail with a generous layer of fresh white Newlyn crab meat. Carefully remove the presentation rings and serve.

Of course, this cocktail can be made without a presentation ring and simply served in a glass of your choice…

…impress your friends by serving this delicious crab cocktail at your summer evening barbecue accompanied by a lovely glass of chilled dry white wine or gorgeous Camel Valley sparkling, just perfect…

Extras

Chilli & Coriander Oil

700ml olive oil
2 red chillis – 1 finely chopped
25g coriander
1 sterilised wine bottle

Take the whole chilli and cut lengthways. Place this chilli into your sterilised bottle. Separate the coriander leaves from the stalks.

Heat the olive oil in a pan until it just starts to simmer and remove from the heat. Place the coriander stalks and the chopped chilli into the hot oil and leave to cool. Once cool, strain the oil through a sieve.

Next, add the coriander leaf to the flavoured oil & transfer into the bottle. Seal the bottle and use at your leisure.

Light Mustard Dressing

1/2 tbsp course grain mustard
1 tbsp Dijon mustard
1/2 tbsp white wine vinegar
300ml olive oil
1 clove of chopped garlic
5g chopped tarragon
1 bay leaf
seasoning
castor sugar - to taste

Place the mustards in a mixing bowl. Add the garlic, tarragon, vinegar, bay leaf and seasoning. Slowly whisk in the olive oil to bring the dressing together. Add sugar at the end to correct the acidity.

Mains

Local Pork Fillet
wrapped in Parma Ham, stuffed with leeks, dates & goats cheese

Serves 4

2 trimmed pork fillets
1 large leek
100g chopped dates
50ml white wine
1 large knob butter

olive oil
seasoning
150g goats cheese
10 slices of Parma ham

Preparing your Pork Fillets

Cut each pork fillet 3/4 depth, lengthways from top to tail. Open the fillet out and cover with cling film. Using either a meat mallet or rolling pin, gently knock the pork fillet to flatten it then remove the cling film. Your pork fillet is then ready for stuffing.

Stuffing, Rolling 'n' Wrapping

Cut the leek in 1/2 lengthways, then chop into 1cm strips. Wash the leek well and dry. In a medium hot pan, add a drizzle of olive oil and sauté the leek for 2 minutes without colour. Add the dates, white wine and butter, and cook for another 3-4 minutes until the dates go slighty "gooey". Remove from the heat and allow to cool.

With each pork fillet laid out, place the stuffing along the centre and full length of each pork fillet. Crumble the goats cheese over the top of the stuffing mix. Roll the pork fillets width ways and away from you, over the stuffing. Keep the roll as tight as possible and the pork fillet will overlap.

Lay 5 slices of Parma ham in a line with the long edges slightly overlapping each other. Place the rolled pork fillet on top of the Parma ham and wrap the Parma ham around the stuffed pork fillet as tightly as possible. Wrap the stuffed pork fillet in cling film and put in the fridge for 1 hour to set. Next, remove the cling film and cut the wrapped and stuffed pork fillet into portions. The size of the pork fillet will determine the size of the portions, but generally one pork fillet will comfortably do two portions. Repeat with the other pork fillet. If your pork fillet does not hold tight, secure with cocktail sticks before cutting into portions and remove after cooking.

Cooking

Oil and season the pork fillets and roast in a medium hot oven for approximately 20 minutes. When cooked, the pork should be firm to the touch, with clear juices running from within. If you used cocktail sticks, remove them to serve.

Cornish Haddock Fillet
with sunblushed tomato, parmesan and basil risotto

Serves 4

4 large haddock fillets (scaled and pin-boned)
150g arborio risotto rice
16 quartered sunblushed tomatoes
50g grated parmesan cheese
10g roughly chopped basil
1 small finely chopped white onion
large knob of butter
vegetable stock
olive oil
100ml white wine
100ml double cream
seasoning

Heat a drizzle of olive oil over a medium heat and sauté the onion and rice for 1-2 minutes. This will start the rice 'working'. Add the sunblushed tomatoes, butter and white wine and cook until almost all of the wine is absorbed by the rice. Gradually add vegetable stock, stir the risotto and simmer, only use the amount of vegetable stock needed for the rice to be almost cooked. Gradually add the double cream, checking the consistency. It should hold its shape and not be too runny. When the rice is cooked, add the parmesan cheese and the basil.

Grill or roast the haddock on a medium to high heat for 6-8 minutes depending on the size of the fillets. When cooked, the fish will be firm to the touch when pressed on the skin side. Serve on top of the hot risotto.

Use the basil risotto as a base to be creative and invent your own flavours. Top risotto with a poached egg for a satisfying Sunday brunch.

...don't underestimate a decent haddock fillet, beautiful – I love it!!

Wild Seabass Fillet
with lemon, vanilla and chive dressing

Serves 4

4 medium to large scaled seabass fillets
4 pak choi
80g fine green beans
1 small leek
8 halved cherry tomatoes
4 sliced radishes
splash of white wine
butter
50g flour
seasoning

Dressing

1 lemon
icing suger
1 vanilla pod
8g finely chopped chives
olive oil
seasoning

Dressing
Remove the skin and segment the lemon. Grill until lightly brown then dust with icing sugar and allow to cool. Scrape 1/2 the vanilla seeds into a bowl along with the chives. Add the lemon segments and any juice, triple the quantity with olive oil and season to taste.

Vegetables
Cut the coarse ends off the fine green beans. Quarter the pak choi and remove the roots. Halve the leek and cut into 1cm diagonal slices. Place a large frying pan over a low heat and drizzle with olive oil. Sauté the green beans for 2 minutes then add the pak choi, leeks and butter. Sauté for a further 3 minutes with a lid on. Remove the lid, increase to a medium heat and add the white wine. Heat until the vegetables are almost cooked. At the last minute, add the radishes and remove from the heat.

Seabass
Heat another large frying pan over a high heat and drizzle with olive oil. Make two small 2cm incisions in the skin side of each fish fillet. This allows even cooking times. Pass the seabass through the seasoned flour and reduce the heat to medium. Cook the fillets for 4 minutes skin side up, flip over and cook for another 4 minutes or until firm to the touch.

To serve, place the seabass filllet on top of the vegetables and drizzle the lemon, vanilla and chive dressing over the fish and around the plate.

Loin of Lamb
with aubergine puree & a roasted garlic & wild mushroom sauce

Serves 4 Loin of Cornish Lamb

Aubergine Puree | 1 aubergine
1 bulb of garlic - 2 cloves
milk
seasoning

Roasted Garlic & Wild Mushroom Sauce | 500ml gravy or lamb stock
150g wild mushrooms
1 tbsp redcurrant jelly
1 tbsp French mustard
1 tbsp tomato puree
300ml red wine
roasted garlic cloves – the rest of the bulb
knob of butter
12g rosemary
seasoning

In this recipe I have used the loin end of lamb, which is the opposite end to the best end of lamb. I have trimmed 2/3 of the outer fat off the lamb, also the fine layer of skin has been removed. If you can't get a butcher to prepare your lamb for you, then you could use whichever cut of lamb is most preferable to you; best end, cutlets… whatever you fancy.

Aubergine Puree | Roast the aubergine in a medium hot oven. After 20 minutes add all of the garlic cloves (in their skins) and roast together for about 10 minutes until both are soft. When the aubergine has cooled, cut in 1/2 lengthways and scrape out the aubergine flesh with a spoon and place in a blender. Peel the garlic cloves, they should be soft and smell beautifully rich. Add two garlic cloves to the aubergine, blend and season. Once the mixture is smooth add milk until you reach your desired consistency. The mixture should just be able to hold itself.

Roast Garlic & Wild Mushroom Sauce | Place your saucepan over a gentle heat, add the red wine, tomato puree, French mustard and redcurrant jelly. Cook down until the ingredients start to thicken, then add the gravy or stock. If you use your own stock, great you'll have to cook the sauce out a bit, and it will need to be thickened using cornflour or arrowroot. Melt butter in a frying pan and gently sauté the mushrooms, rosemary and seasoning until just cooked. Add the remaining roasted garlic cloves. Introduce the mushroom mix to the sauce. Cook out the sauce for 5 minutes, so that the mushroom and garlic flavours infuse the sauce. Your sauce is now ready to serve.

Cooking your Lamb | Cut the lamb into noisettes and pan sear in a hot pan for 2 minutes on each side. Finish in the oven or under the grill for 6-7 minutes. Cook to your liking, around medium rare is best.

…I love the flavour of lamb! Use the cut of meat that you are most familiar with, put your time into the sauce & play with the flavours… this is a great sauce for roast lamb.

Aubergine, Spinach & Ricotta Cannelloni
with sweet & sour vegetables

Serves 4

Aubergine Cannelloni	3 aubergines 100g spinach 50g ricotta cheese 12g chopped basil 2 finely chopped shallots seasoning	Sweet & Sour Sauce	2 tsp tomato puree 100g castor sugar 200ml white wine vinegar 1 garlic clove 40g ginger soy sauce Worcestershire sauce 100ml pineapple juice juice of 1/2 lime
Mediterranean Vegetables	1 large chopped courgette 1 large chopped red onion 3 chunky cut peppers 2 chunky cut tomatoes		

Aubergine Cannelloni | Cut the aubergine into long thin strips. The strips must be the full length of the aubergine, 12 in total. Brush the aubergine strips with olive oil and season. Char-grill the aubergine strips until supple. In a hot pan, sweat the shallots down, without colour, for 2 minutes. Add the spinach and a lid. After approximately 1 minute, when the spinach has wilted, remove from the pan and place in a mixing bowl to cool. When cool add the ricotta and basil leaves, season and mix well. Lay the aubergine strips out on a flat surface. Place a spoonful of the ricotta mix on the centre of the strip and roll up tightly so that the ends overlap to form the base of the cannelloni. Cook the cannelloni for 10-15 minutes in a hot oven.

Sweet & Sour Sauce | Add sugar, white wine vinegar, tomato puree, garlic, ginger, soy sauce and Worcestershire sauce to a medium hot pan. Cook down gently until the ingredients become syrupy. Add both the pineapple and lime juice. Season well and cook down again to a nice sticky consistency

Mediterranean Vegetables | Place the courgette, red onion, peppers and tomatoes into a roasting pan. Season the vegetables and drizzle with olive oil. Roast the vegetables in a medium hot oven for 15-20 minutes. Then add to the sweet and sour sauce until nicely coated.

…this dish is fantastic served with fennel seed scented pilau rice or chunky potato wedges & sour cream…

Extras

Basil Pesto Dressing

10g pine nuts
10g garlic
10g parmesan cheese
100g basil
50g spinach
seasoning
olive oil

Blend all of the dry ingredients. Add the olive oil to create the desired consistency.

Creamy Leeks

80ml white wine
200ml cream
100g leeks
seasoning

In a small saucepan, add the white wine and reduce. Add the cream and bring to the boil. Cut the leeks lengthways and slice. Once boiling, add the leeks and season. Cook out until the leeks have softened and the sauce is thick & bubbling.

...the variations to this are endless, you could add meats such as bacon, pancetta, chorizo, you will need to cook these before adding to the sauce. Also shallots, sun-blushed tomatoes and fresh cut herbs, make a great sauce. My favourite combination being shallots & tarragon, as these bring out the flavour of the leeks fantastically well.

Desserts

Arty's Honeycomb Parfait

Serves 6

Honeycomb	40g clear honey	Parfait	1 egg
	70g liquid glucose		50g castor sugar
	200g castor sugar		150ml double cream
	10g bicarbonate of soda		
	3 tbsp of water		
	parchment paper		

Honeycomb | Line a large shallow baking tray with baking parchment. Place the honey and glucose into a heavy-based saucepan, add the sugar and water. Gently heat until the sugar dissolves. Then increase the heat to medium and stir occasionally. When the edges start to turn a light golden caramel colour 148°C stir in the bicarbonate of soda. Be careful when adding the bicarbonate of soda as it will erupt like crazy and it is very hot! Pour the mixture onto the parchment paper. Allow the honeycomb to cool for 1 hour until crunchy. Break up into small pieces.

Parfait | Line a triangle mould or small ice cream tub with cling film, alternatively you could make small cones from parchment paper.

Add the egg and sugar to a mixing bowl. Place the mixing bowl over a bowl of hot water and whisk the egg and sugar together until they become thick and creamy. An electric whisk is ideal for this. Whip the cold double cream until it holds a firm peak. Fold the whipped cream and 1/3 of the honeycomb pieces into the egg and sugar mixture and place into the mould or container. Place in the freezer for 4-5 hours. Serve with summer berries and honeycomb pieces.

You could cover the parfait with the chocolate glaze (see page 60) and freeze like an ice cream 'crunchie' bar, or serve with vanilla sauce and fresh berry coulis (see page 66).

Store the rest of the honeycomb in an airtight container for next time, you will definitely make this recipe again…

…you will always be the King (or Queen) of dinner parties with this parfait…

Citrus Cheesecake

Makes a 30cm diameter cheesecake

Base | 250g digestive biscuits
75g butter
1 tbsp castor sugar

Topping | 500g soft cream cheese
225g sugar
1/2 tsp vanilla essence
zest of 1 lemon
zest & juice of 2 limes
1 tbsp lemon juice
3 egg yolks
200ml sour cream
500ml double cream
5 leaves of gelatine

Base
Blend the biscuits until they form a fine crumb and add the sugar. Gently melt the butter in a pan. Add the biscuit mix to the butter and mix well. Line a 30cm cake tin with greaseproof paper on the bottom and 5cm around the side. Place the biscuit mixture into the tin and press it out using the back of a spoon, until it is well compressed and of equal depth throughout. Place in the fridge to chill.

Filling
Place the gelatine leaves into a small bowl of cold water and ensure that they are fully soaked. Place the cream cheese, sugar, vanilla essence, egg yolks, sour cream and lemon and lime zest into a mixing bowl. Whisk until evenly blended. Whisk the double cream in a separate bowl until soft but still runny.

Heat up the lemon and lime juice over a low heat. Remove from the heat. Take the gelatine leaves from the water and squeeze out any excess moisture. Add to the warm juice and dissolve. Pour onto the cream cheese mixture and mix gently. Add the whipped cream and fold through. Take the biscuit base from the fridge and pour the mixture over the top. Level out the top and return to the fridge for 6-8 hours.

To serve sprinkle a little lemon and lime zest onto the top of the cheescake and accompany with fresh berry coulis (see page 66) and clotted cream.

Rich Chocolate Roulade

Serves 4-6

Chocolate Sponge	90g castor sugar 5 eggs 60g plain flour 40g cocoa powder

Chocolate glaze	125g broken dark chocolate 75g liquid glucose 125ml double cream 1 tbsp vegetable oil

Chocolate Cream	150g broken dark chocolate 65ml milk 55g butter 1 egg yolk 235ml double cream 20g castor sugar

Chocolate Sponge | Whisk the sugar and eggs together until they have doubled in volume. Sift the flour and cocoa powder over the egg mixture and fold in until smooth. Line a large baking sheet with greaseproof paper. Spread the mixture onto the greaseproof paper approximately 1cm thick. Bake for 10-12 minutes at 180°C until just firm. Leave to cool.

Chocolate Cream | Add milk and butter to a thick bottomed pan and bring to the boil. Remove from the heat and stir in the chocolate pieces until smooth. Set aside. Whisk the egg yolk and sugar. Then fold the chocolate mixture into the egg yolk and sugar. Cool to room temperature. Half whip the double cream and fold into the chocolate mix.

Assembling your Roulade | Take a clean sheet of greaseproof paper and sprinkle evenly with castor sugar. Lay the sponge face down on the greaseproof paper and peel off the original greaseproof paper. Cover the sponge evenly with chocolate cream, approximately 1cm thick. Fold the edge of the sponge into the chocolate cream. Then roll using the greaseproof paper, ensuring that the sponge is tucked in evenly along the length. Try and keep the roll as tight as possible until completely rolled, and evenly round. Leave wrapped in greaseproof paper and place in fridge for one hour to set the cream.

Chocolate Glaze | Heat the cream and glucose in a pan to simmering point. Pour cream mixture over the chocolate and stir until smooth. Stir in the oil.

Glazing the Rich Chocolate Roulade | Place a layer of cling film on a clean work surface. Then place a cooling wire rack on top. Unwrap your roulade from the greaseproof paper and place on the wire rack. Spoon the chocolate glaze onto the roulade until completely coated. Place in fridge for 20 minutes to set. Serve whole or sliced into portions. The excess chocolate on the cling film can be used again.

…don't forget your Cornish clotted cream or ice cream…

'the cove' Eton Mess

Serves 6

6 meringue nests
50g raspberries
50g quartered strawberries
50g de-stoned black cherries
25g redcurrants
25g blackcurrants
25g blueberries

2 tbsp elderflower cordial
juice of 1/2 lemon
zest of 1/4 lemon
55g castor sugar
225ml double cream
50g greek yoghurt
6 dessert glasses

Place all of the fresh berries into a bowl and mix with half of the elderflower cordial, lemon zest, lemon juice and 35g of castor sugar. The liquid should just about coat all of the berries. Gently mix the berries to break their skins. Marinate for 1 hour.

Break up the meringue nests into small chunks. Whisk together the double cream, greek yoghurt, rest of the elderflower cordial and 20g of castor sugar until it forms soft peaks and place in the fridge.

Spoon a little of the whipped cream into each dessert glass. Press a handful of the meringue into the cream. Add a generous spoonful of berries to each glass, but do not add too much juice. Repeat and layer the mixtures until the glasses are full.

Drizzle the fruit syrup over the final layer and finish with a little extra cream.

Triple Chocolate Mousse

Serves 10

300ml milk
6 egg yolks
12g castor sugar
6 leaves gelatine
400ml whipped double cream
100ml egg white
100g broken white chocolate
100g broken milk chocolate
100g broken dark chocolate

Fully submerge the gelatine leaves in a small bowl of cold water.

Add the milk to a pan and simmer gently on a low heat. Whisk the egg yolks and sugar together. Slowly pour the warm milk into the egg and sugar mix, whisking continuously. Return the mixture to the heat and stir gently with a wooden spoon until the mixture thickens and coats the back of the spoon, like custard. Do not let the mixture boil. Take the gelatine leaves from the water and squeeze out any excess moisture. Add the gelatine to the warm mixture and leave to dissolve.

Put each 100g of chocolate into separate mixing bowls. Divide the warm custard mix equally between the three bowls. Stir each mixture with a clean spoon until the chocolate is fully melted and has blended evenly. Spoon 1/3 of the whipped cream into the dark chocolate mixture and gently fold. Use an electric mixer to whisk the egg whites. Add 1/3 of the egg white mix and again gently fold until evenly mixed. Repeat for the bowls of white and milk chocolate.

Using the chocolate sponge recipe (see page 60) cut 10 discs, roughly 1/2cm thick, to fit the bottom of the lined 7cm diameter presentation rings. Pour the dark chocolate mixture into the lined presentation rings to form the first layer of your mousse. Place in the fridge to set. When set, repeat the process with the milk chocolate and then again with the white chocolate to create your layers. Drizzle the chocolate glaze (see page 60) on top of the final layer.

Alternatively the mousses can be presented in beautiful glasses, no need for the chocolate sponge base. The chocolate mixtures may begin to set before you add the cream and meringue mixtures. If this occurs place the jug into a tray or bowl of warm water and stir gently with a wooden spoon. These individual mousses can be frozen for up to 1 month.

...real chocoholics will be tempted to use chocolate brownie for the base...

Extras

Raspberry Coulis

225g fresh or frozen raspberries
juice of 1/2 lemon
250g sugar
200ml water

Boil the sugar and water until syrupy. Add raspberries and lemon juice. Blend the mix in a food processor and then sieve to remove seeds. Keep refrigerated until required.

Sauce Anglaise

4 egg yolks
75g castor sugar
300ml milk
1/2 vanilla pod

Whisk the egg yolks and 1/3 of the sugar. Combine the milk, split vanilla pod and remaining sugar in a saucepan and bring to the boil. Pour the milk onto the egg yolks and whisk. Pour back into the pan, remove the vanilla pod and cook out over a low heat until it coats the back of the spoon. DO NOT BOIL! Set aside to cool.

...if you boil the mix you will split your sauce anglaise & will have something that resembles scrambled eggs! Start again.

Acknowledgements

Persistent hard work from all of my kitchen team over the last five years have meant that this cookbook has been able to materialise, my express gratitude goes out especially to Dave, Marco and Sticky who have contributed so much through some extremely testing times to make both the restaurant a success and this cookbook a possibility... thank you guys and "head down, keep going!!!". A big plus to the team is you J9, bringing your exceptional skills and experience to the pastry section and being a cornerstone in our operational kitchen. I'm sure that she would like to dedicate her input of recipes to her gorgeous baby boy Rohan... congratulations J9 and Matt. More thanks to Claire for your creativity, able participation in the project and dedication in making this cookbook a reality... and to everyone who has helped me, past and present, cheers to you all...

However, without Mads this cookbook would not have happened – your university project and an enormous amount of patience has seen this cookbook through from conception to creation... your eye for detail, persistent enthusiasm (admittedly, sometimes feeling like a continual battering alongside the running of a busy restaurant) and your drive for perfection has made this cookbook. Any less of a professional would have run for the hills (or London!) and I feel incredibly lucky that it was you Mads who took the project (and me) on...thanks, thanks, thanks Mads, you beauty....

Finally to Net, thank you for all your hard work and support over the years. I can't say how much I appreciate all that you have done to help me complete the book, your input within the restaurant and how lucky I am to have you by my side both professionally and personally, you do an amazing job - just to say thank you and I love you lots and lots.

'the cove' . maenporth beach . nr falmouth . cornwall . tr11 5hn
01326 251136
www.thecovemaenporth.co.uk